KATHRY   for children
of all   *onrise*,
was publi   SCO Prize
for Servi   her story
Somethi   She has
worked in   tly was an
Editorial   to become
a full-tim   *Takes the*
Plung   ffin);
The Emperoi   *d* (Hodder)
and *The*   d titles
for Franc   previous

For Isis and Makeda – K.C.

First published in Great Britain in 2002 by
Frances Lincoln Limited, 4 Torriano Mews,
Torriano Avenue, London NW5 2RZ

First paperback edition 2002

British Library Cataloguing in Publication Data available on request

ISBN 978-0-7112-1910-6

Printed in Jurong Town, Singapore by Star Standard Industries in October 2009

7 9 8

*Oxfam and the publishers would like to thank Nothando and her family, their community in Nkandla district,
KwaZulu Natal and Kwazi Mazibuko for their enthusiastic support.*

*Oxfam GB will receive a 5% royalty for each copy of this book sold in the UK.
Oxfam is a Registered Charity no. 202918. Oxfam GB is a member of Oxfam International.*

*Oxfam believes every human being is entitled to a life of dignity and opportunity. Working with others we
use our ingenuity, knowledge and wealth of experience to make resources and money work harder.
From practical work with individuals through to influencing world policy we aim to enable the world's
poorest people to create a future that no longer needs Oxfam.*

ONE CHILD ONE SEED

A SOUTH AFRICAN COUNTING BOOK

Kathryn Cave • *Photographs by* Gisèle Wulfsohn

FRANCES LINCOLN
In Association with Oxfam

One child, one seed.

Here is Nothando with her pumpkin seed.
She lives in South Africa, where pumpkins grow all summer long.

Nothando lives with her Aunt Nomusa (in red) and her Grandmother Betty (in blue). Her big sister and her mother are on the right of the picture, and her brother is on the left. They live nearby and spend a lot of time with Nothando.

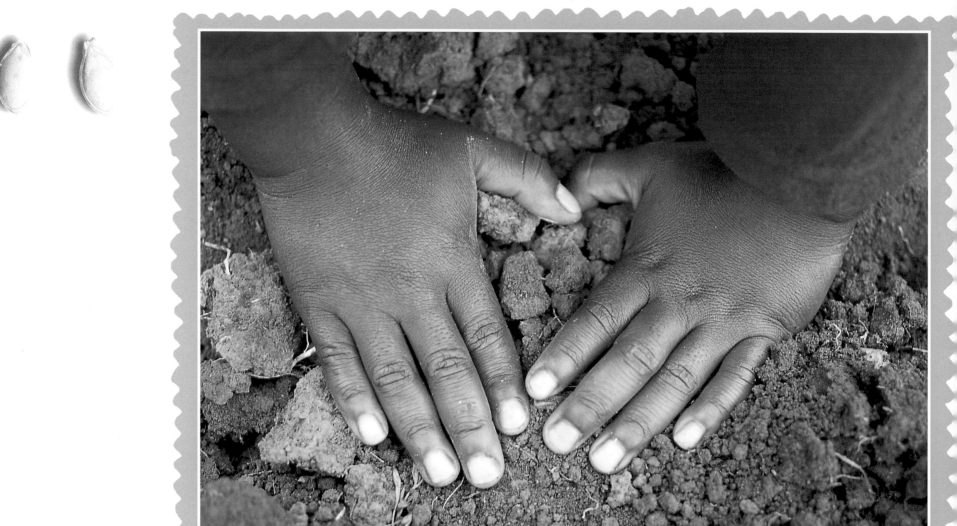

2 **Two** hands to plant the seed.

Nothando buries the pumpkin seed in the earth. It's November, the beginning of summer. The summer rains will help the seed to grow. By February, it will have grown into a pumpkin big enough to eat.

The homestead where Nothando lives is in a district called Nkandla. The main house has a kitchen, a living room and a bedroom.

Its walls (shown in the picture) are made of wood, mud and grass. They are then plastered and painted. The roof is corrugated iron. Outside there are three thatched huts called rondavels, used for cooking and storage.

3 Three ways to help it grow.

Nothando's brother Siphelele has a spade to dig up weeds. Their friend Nobuhle has water in her bucket to keep the little plant alive in dry weather. Nothando helps with the hoe.

Some years the summer rains are very heavy, and the river that flows through Nkandla floods. Too much water is bad for the crops: they rot, and when the water finally drains away there's lots of clearing up to do. Women do the work by hand, with help from the children.

Four creatures watch.

If these cows get too close they'll tread on the little pumpkin plant, or even eat it.

Who will see that they don't? Nothando's cousin Mongezi gets that job. He's the family cowherd.

All the animals on the homestead have to earn their keep. Cows do that by giving milk and meat. Chicks provide eggs and meat once they're fully grown. Cats and dogs make themselves useful by chasing and catching rats.

5

Five friends to pick the pumpkin.

Any month can be harvest time because vegetables grow all year round. Out in the fields and in the vegetable garden you can find cabbage, spinach, beetroot, potatoes, beans and mealies (the local name for maize).

The pumpkin's stalk has dried out. That means the pumpkin's ripe. It's time for Nothando and her friends to pick it and carry it home.

Six things to buy.

Sibongile store is a ten-minute walk from the homestead. The town of Nkandla is much further, and there aren't many shops there – just a few that sell food or clothes. There's a farmers' market in the town, too.

Now it's time to turn the pumpkin into a feast! Nothando walks to the store to stock up with sugar, mealie meal, bread and margarine, and a passionfruit drink. The curry powder is for a vegetable curry, tomorrow.

7 **Seven** weary walkers.

It's a long walk home for dinner after an afternoon in the vegetable garden. But that's the way most people get around here: on foot.

The roads around Nkandla are just dirt, and in the rainy season they can't be used. When it's not too wet, this small van runs a taxi service three times a day from outside Nothando's school into town and back again. The half-hour trip costs 6 rand each way.

The nearest big city is Durban, 300 km away. Nothando dreams of going there one day.

Eight slices of ripe pumpkin.

Tonight Aunt Nomusa is chief cook. First she cuts off the pumpkin's tough peel. Then she scrapes out the seeds, and cuts the pumpkin into slices. It looks a lot smaller now – let's hope there's enough to go round.

Aunt Nomusa adds mealie meal to the cooked pumpkin to thicken it, and sugar to make it sweet. The homestead has no fridge, so fresh food has to be cooked and eaten before it goes bad.

Many families can't afford to cook more than once a day, usually in the evening. Those who can, cook lunch or a midday snack too: bean soup or chicken and mealie meal. Breakfast is usually a mug of tea and some bread.

9 Nine hungry eaters waiting for a treat

Games make the time until dinner pass more quickly. This is Am I In?, Nothando's favourite. You mark out squares on the ground, and hop round kicking a stone from square to square. If the stone misses the right square, you're out.

Most of the games here use objects that cost nothing, like sticks and stones.

Nomusa is cooking a big pot of a traditional Zulu dish: 'isijingi'. Tonight the weather's hot, so she prepares the meal outside. Everyone stops to watch.

10

Ten dinner plates piled high.

It's dinner time at last. And there's plenty for everyone!

When the meal is over, the children clear away. They wash up under the cold tap beside the house, scrubbing the plates with their hands or a wet cloth until they are clean again.

The isijingi's gone now, every bit. There's just one part of the pumpkin left. Can you guess what it is?

 **1** One child, one seed to plant next time

1	one
2	two
3	three
4	four
5	five
6	six
7	seven
8	eight
9	nine
10	ten

More About South Africa

South Africa lies at the southern tip of the great continent of Africa. Nkandla, where Nothando lives, is in the north east of the country, about 50 miles from the Indian Ocean.

Tiny measurements on this map represent great distances in real life. South Africa is five times the size of Britain and more than 41 million people live there. The whole continent of Africa measures more than four thousand miles from north to south. The map shows 8 of Africa's 54 countries.

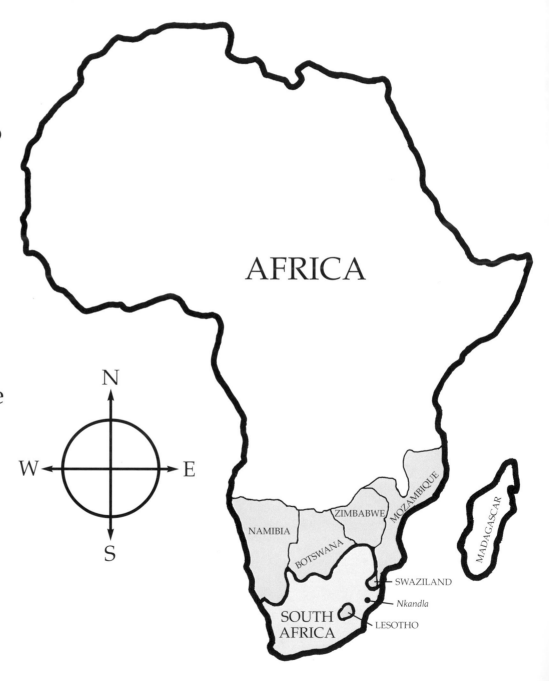

Pumpkin Pie

Pumpkins can be cooked in lots of different ways. Pumpkin pie is a sweet dish that is eaten at Thanksgiving in the USA.

INGREDIENTS

250 g (8 oz) shortcrust pastry • 1 small pumpkin, weighing about 1.15 kg (2 ¾ lb)
2 eggs • 1 tin (400 g) sweetened condensed milk
1 teaspoon ground cinnamon • ½ teaspoon ground ginger
½ teaspoon ground nutmeg • ½ teaspoon salt

METHOD

1. Scoop the flesh out of the pumpkin, throwing away the skin and seeds.
2. Put the flesh in a pan, cover with water and simmer for 25 minutes, until tender.
3. Drain and leave to cool, then purée it in a blender or mash it, until it is free of lumps.
4. Preheat the oven to 200°C (400°F, Gas Mark 6)
5. Roll out the pastry on a lightly-floured work surface and use to line a 23 cm (9 inch) pie dish. Cover with greaseproof paper, fill with rice or baking beans and bake for 10 minutes.
6. Remove the paper and rice or beans, and return the dish to the oven for 5 minutes until the pastry is golden brown. Remove from the oven and reduce the heat to 190°C (375°F, Gas Mark 5).
7. In a large bowl, combine the pumpkin purée, eggs and sweetened condensed milk. Add the cinnamon, ginger, nutmeg and salt. Whisk together until thoroughly blended.
8. Pour into the pastry case and bake for 40 minutes until a knife inserted comes out clean.
9. Serve with whipped cream.

MORE TITLES FROM
FRANCES LINCOLN CHILDREN'S BOOKS
IN ASSOCIATION WITH OXFAM

W is for World
Kathryn Cave

Stunning colour images from around the world invite
children to focus on the similarities as well as the differences
between other cultures and their own.

ISBN 978-1-84507-314-5

Wake Up, World!
A Day in the Life of Children Across the Globe
Beatrice Hollyer

Meet eight children from around the world as they eat,
play, go to school and talk about their dreams for the future.

ISBN 978-0-7112-1484-2

Let's Eat!
Children and their Food Around the World
Beatrice Hollyer

Meet five children, one each from Thailand, South Africa,
India, France and Mexico, and find out where their food comes from,
whether they buy it or grow it themselves and especially
what they like and dislike.

ISBN 978-1-84507-329-9

Frances Lincoln titles are available from all good bookshops.
You can also buy books and find out more about your favourite titles,
authors and illustrators on our website: www.franceslincoln.com